Office of the Special Project Facilitator's

Lessons Learned

Sri Lanka Clean Energy and Network Efficiency Investment Project

ADB

ISBN 978-92-9262-106-3 (print), 978-92-9262-107-0 (electronic), 978-92-9262-108-7 (ebook)
Publication Stock No. ARM200272-2
DOI: http://dx.doi.org/10.22617/ARM200272-2

The views expressed in this publication are those of the authors and do not necessarily reflect the views and policies of the Asian Development Bank (ADB) or its Board of Governors or the governments they represent.

ADB does not guarantee the accuracy of the data included in this publication and accepts no responsibility for any consequence of their use. The mention of specific companies or products of manufacturers does not imply that they are endorsed or recommended by ADB in preference to others of a similar nature that are not mentioned.

By making any designation of or reference to a particular territory or geographic area, or by using the term "country" in this document, ADB does not intend to make any judgments as to the legal or other status of any territory or area.

Please contact pubsmarketing@adb.org if you have questions or comments with respect to content, or if you wish to obtain copyright permission for your intended use that does not fall within these terms, or for permission to use the ADB logo.

Corrigenda to ADB publications may be found at http://www.adb.org/publications/corrigenda.

Notes:
In this publication, "$" refers to United States dollars and "SLRs" refers to Sri Lankan rupees.

ADB recognizes "Ceylon" as Sri Lanka.

On the cover: The project aims to support development of clean energy, to strengthen the transmission and distribution network, and to improve system reliability and reduce technical losses (photo by SLRM).

Contents

Map

Acknowledgments

The Office of the Special Project Facilitator's (OSPF) *Lessons Learned* series featuring Sri Lanka's Clean Energy and Network Efficiency Investment Project is a collaborative effort led by Sushma Kotagiri, principal facilitation specialist, OSPF, and Ranishka Yasanga Wimalasena, energy specialist, Pacific Department (PARD) [formerly with Sri Lanka Resident Mission (SLRM)]. Chamindra Weerackody, OSPF consultant, contributed to the research and preliminary writing. The case study greatly benefited from the contributions, comments, discussions, and support of various professionals—Malraj Fernando and Thuiyalage Sandasiri, project managers, Ceylon Electricity Board; Manjula Amerasinghe, principal environment specialist, East Asia Department (former officer-in-charge, SLRM); Prathaj Haputhanthri, associate project officer (energy), SLRM; Mary Jane David, senior consultation officer, OSPF (content and structure); Wilfredo Agliam, associate facilitation coordinator, OSPF (administration and coordination with all the participating agencies and stakeholders); Joy Gatmaytan (editor); and Michelle Ortiz (design and layout).

The team greatly appreciates the advice and guidance received from Warren Evans, special project facilitator, OSPF; Sri Widowati, former country director, SLRM; and Chen Chen, country director, SLRM, during the analytical work and publication process.

Abbreviations

ADB	–	Asian Development Bank
AP	–	affected people
AM	–	Accountability Mechanism
CEB	–	Ceylon Electricity Board
CENEIP	–	Clean Energy and Network Efficiency Improvement Project
DAS	–	Department of Agrarian Services
DOA	–	Department of Archaeology
DOW	–	Department of Wildlife
DSD	–	Divisional Secretary's Division
GND	–	Grama Niladhari Division
GRM	–	grievance redress mechanism
ha	–	hectare
km	–	kilometer
kV	–	kilovolt
OSPF	–	Office of the Special Project Facilitator
PUCSL	–	Public Utilities Commission of Sri Lanka
ROW	–	right of way
SLR	–	Sri Lanka rupee

I. Introduction

The Asian Development Bank (ADB) envisions a prosperous, inclusive, resilient, and sustainable Asia and the Pacific, while sustaining its efforts to eradicate extreme poverty in the region. It assists its members and partners by providing loans, technical assistance, grants, and equity investments to promote social and economic development.

ADB maximizes the development impact of its assistance by facilitating policy dialogues, providing advisory services, and mobilizing financial resources through cofinancing operations that tap official, commercial, and export credit sources.

Excavation and construction works by the project (photo by OSPF).

Accountability Mechanism

Development effectiveness requires high standards of accountability, transparency, openness, and public participation. As an international development agency dedicated to eliminating poverty in Asia and the Pacific, ADB constantly strives to enhance these aspects in its operations. It thus established the Accountability Mechanism (AM) that provides a forum where people adversely affected by ADB-assisted projects can voice and seek solutions to their problems and report what may be noncompliance with ADB's operational policies and procedures.

The AM is designed to:[1]

- increase ADB's development effectiveness and project quality;

- be responsive to the concerns of project-affected people and fair to all stakeholders;

- reflect the highest professional and technical standards in its staffing and operations;

- be as independent and transparent as possible; and

- be cost-effective, efficient, and complementary to the other supervision, audit, quality control, and evaluation systems at ADB.

The AM consists of two separate but complementary functions: problem-solving and compliance review.

The problem-solving function, under the Office of the Special Project Facilitator (OSPF), focuses on finding satisfactory solutions to problems caused by ADB-assisted projects. The compliance review function, under the Office of the Compliance Review Panel, focuses on whether projects comply with ADB's operational policies and procedures that affect or may affect local people directly, materially, and adversely. Both offices ensure that the mechanism is known and understood within and outside ADB through different avenues including outreach activities.

ADB remains firmly committed to the principle of being accountable for complying with its operational policies and procedures, and solving problems of project-affected people. Therefore, it intends to ensure that the AM remains adequate and effective in keeping with current international best practices.

Safeguard Policy Statement

The ADB Safeguard Policy Statement (SPS) 2009 is the set of operational policies that seeks to prevent adverse impact of projects to the environment and society. The policy framework consists of guidelines on the environment, involuntary resettlement, and indigenous peoples.

---

[1]   ADB. 2012. *Accountability Mechanism Policy.* Manila.

The safeguard requirements are put into place to ensure that throughout the project cycle, the following are done: (i) identification and assessment of possible project impacts, (ii) development and implementation of action plans to minimize and mitigate the negative impacts of a project and to compensate the affected people (AP) in case negative impacts cannot be avoided, and (iii) conduct of meaningful consultations with AP so that they are informed on the impacts from project preparation through implementation.

Throughout the years and because of experience with different projects, the SPS has been enhanced to strengthen its framework. The current safeguards aim to respond to the changing requirements of clients while ensuring the long-term sustainability of the systems. The best practices of other multilateral financial institutions are incorporated or are being incorporated in the frameworks to ensure that other social dimensions (e.g., gender issues and labor standards) are taken into consideration, that there is better harmony of the policies among different financial institutions, and that the scope of the policies are clearer and better monitored to ensure accountability.[2]

Grievance Redress Mechanism

A grievance redress mechanism (GRM) is a combination of institutions, instruments, methods, and processes by which resolution of a grievance is sought and provided.[3] It is intended to provide a predictable, transparent, and credible process to all parties, resulting in outcomes that are fair, effective, and lasting.[4] This facilitates resolution of AP's concerns and grievances about the borrower's/client's social and environmental performance at the project level. The GRM should be scaled to the risks and impacts of the project and should address AP's concerns and complaints promptly, using an understandable and transparent process that is gender responsive, culturally appropriate, and readily accessible to all segments of the AP (footnote 2).

*A grievance redress mechanism is a combination of institutions, instruments, methods, and processes by which **resolution of a grievance is sought and provided.***

---

[2]   ADB. 2009. *Safeguard Policy Statement.* Manila.
[3]   Center for European Policy Analysis. 2009. *A Review of the Southern Transport Development Project.* Colombo.
[4]   International Finance Corporation. 2008. *Advisory Note: A Guide to Designing and Implementing Grievance Mechanisms for Development Projects.* Washington, DC.

Methodology of the Study

OSPF conducted analytical work of selected GRMs and problem-solving processes established by ADB-assisted projects in their respective countries.

The objectives of the case study are to:

(i) review the institutional arrangements and processes established by ADB-assisted projects for handling grievances and complaints reported by APs during project planning and implementation;

(ii) assess the efficiency and effectiveness of the GRMs in grievance handling, and identify the lessons learned and the good practices in grievance redress that can be replicated in similar contexts;

(iii) produce a knowledge product based on empirical evidences elicited from the case study that will provide valuable insights and guidance to project-based grievance redress processes; and

(iv) use the case study for developing training materials that could be shared at OSPF training programs for GRM practitioners and project-implementing agencies.

In consultation with the Sri Lanka Resident Mission (SLRM), OSPF selected two projects for the studies, one of which is the Clean Energy and Network Efficiency Improvement Project (CENEIP) implemented by the Ceylon Electricity Board (CEB).

The case study approach was largely qualitative. Document reviews, secondary data collection, and individual interviews conducted with selected project staff and consultants and the complainants constituted the key components of the methodology adopted for the case study. Secondary data on the implementation of GRMs and problem-solving processes were drawn from project-related documents such as samples of written complaints that described grievances as well as those showing compensation paid by the project to the APs (Thulhiriya–Kegalle transmission line); a Microsoft PowerPoint presentation used for raising awareness among divisional secretaries and other government agencies; and various instruments used to (i) receive clearance for the right of way (ROW) of the transmission line from the project-affected people and other relevant government agencies, (ii) assess compensation for the affected trees and properties, and (iii) record payment of compensation to APs. Interviews were conducted with the project managers of the two transmission line projects, and 10 complainants of the Anuradhapura–Mannar transmission line.

II. The Project: Clean Energy and Network Efficiency Investment Project

CENEIP was to support development of clean energy; to strengthen the transmission and distribution network, especially in conflict-affected areas of northern and eastern provinces; and to improve system reliability and reduce technical losses. The project was expected to contribute to a reliable, adequate, and affordable power supply for sustainable economic growth and poverty reduction. The anticipated outcomes of the project were increased clean power supply, and improved efficiency and reliability of delivery of electricity. The project had three major outputs: (i) transmission infrastructure development in Northern Province; (ii) transmission and distribution network efficiency improvement; and (iii) solar rooftop power generation pilot that would integrate renewable energy sources into the grid. CEB was the project implementing agency for outputs 1 and 2, and the Sri Lanka Sustainable Energy Authority was the implementing agency for output 3.[5] The project commenced in 2013 and was planned to be completed in December 2016. The loan was to close in June 2017, however, due to unforeseen reasons, all outputs could not be realized by project closure, thus, a 2-year extension was granted.

Men at work on the transmission line (photo by SLRM).

---

[5] ADB. 2012. *Report and Recommendation of the President to the Board of Directors: Proposed Loans, Technical Assistance Grant, and Administration of Grant to the Democratic Socialist Republic of Sri Lanka for the Clean Energy and Network Efficiency Improvement Project.* Manila.

SRI LANKA
CLEAN ENERGY AND NETWORK EFFICIENCY IMPROVEMENT PROJECT (CENEIP)

Palk Strait

Kankasanturai

Kodikamam

Jaffna

Palk Bay

Kilinochchi

Mullaittivu

Tanniyuttu

Mankulam

NORTHERN

Talaimannar

Puliyankulam

Mannar

Mannar

Gulf of Mannar

Horowupotana

◉ **Trincomalee**

Anuradhapura

Periyanagavillu

New Anuradhapura

NORTH CENTRAL

Bay of Bengal

Tambuttegama

Kekirawa

Welikanda

Puttalam

Polonnaruwa

Valaichchenai

Dambulla

EASTERN

Batticaloa

NORTH WESTERN

CENTRAL

Chilaw

Matale

Ampara

Madampe

Kurunegala ◉

Thulhiriya

◉ **Kandy**

Kegalle

Kegalle

Negombo

Gampola

Katunayake

Gampaha

Talawakele

Nuwara Eliya

Badulla ◉

Welimada

Colombo

Avissawella

SRI JAYAWARDENEPURA KOTTE

UVA

Moratuwa

Hatton

Bandarawela

Monaragala

WESTERN

◉ **Ratnapura**

Wellawaya

Kalutara

Pelmadulla

Balangoda

SABARAGAMUWA

Alutgama

Elpitiya

Ambalangoda

SOUTHERN

Hikkaduwa

Akuressa

Hambantota

Galle

Tangalle

Matara

INDIAN OCEAN

Legend

Symbol	Description
▬	132 kV Transmission Line
▬	220 kV Transmission Line
⚡	Grid Substation
⊛	National Capital
◉	Chief Provincial Town
●	City/Town
	District Boundary
	Provincial Boundary
kV	kilovolt

Boundaries are not necessarily authoritative.

0 10 20 30 40 50
Kilometers

N

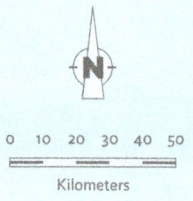

The case study of CENEIP focused on two of its transmission line projects: the 220-kilovolt (kV) transmission line from Anuradhapura to Mannar and the 132 kV transmission line from Thulhiriya to Kegalle.

Anuradhapura–Mannar 220-Kilovolt Transmission Line

Description

Work for this project commenced in May 2015. The total length of the Anuradhapura–Mannar 220 kV transmission line was 138 kilometers (km), traversing 10 Divisional Secretary's Divisions (DSDs) and 3 districts in the dry and arid (Mannar) zones of Sri Lanka: Anuradhapura, Vavuniya, and Mannar. The last two fell within the former conflict-affected region.

In the Anuradhapura district, forests, shrubs,[6] and large inland water bodies occupy nearly 60% of the total land and paddy cultivation; home gardens, and perennial and other seasonal crops areas account for another 38%. The estimated population in the district is 929,539 a significant proportion of which are the families resettled under the Mahaweli development scheme. Around 94% of the population is rural, largely dependent on rain-fed paddy cultivation during maha

season (north–east monsoon period from September to March) followed by cultivation of other highland crops during the yala season from May to end-August. The land consumption per household is 3.1 hectares (ha) and the population density is 129 per square km.[7]

Forest reserves constitute almost half of the total land of the Vavuniya district and shrubs occupy 6%. Several large reservoirs in the district are the source of water for agricultural activities. The cultivated areas—paddy, home gardens, and perennial and seasonal crops comprise—fill 37% of the district's land area, which has an estimated population of 187,310 of which 80% is in the rural area. Land consumption per household is 4.2 ha and the population density is 95 per square km.[8]

In the Mannar district, forest reserves comprise around 76% of the total land area. A significant population in the district is engaged in marine and inland fishing industry; hence, the cultivated area is limited to around 16%. This area includes home gardens, paddy cultivations, and those planted with perennial and seasonal crops. Of the population of 109,211, 75% live in rural areas. Household land consumption is 7.5 ha, and the population density is 55 per square km.[9]

The transmission line traversed urban and peri-urban areas such as Mihintale, Anuradhapura, Rambewa, Madawachchiya, Vavuniya, and Mannar; settlements; and built-up areas. To avoid settlements, forest

---

6   Shrub lands are illegally cleared by farmers for slash-and-burn agriculture (*chenas*).
7   Department of Census and Statistics. 2018. District Statistical Handbook for Anuradhapura.
8   Department of Census and Statistics. 2018. District Statistical Handbook for Vavuniya.
9   Department of Census and Statistics. 2018. District Statistical Handbook for Mannar.

*The project ensured **giving adequate time for people to raise their objections.***

areas were preferred for the ROW. However, forest reserves and wildlife sanctuaries in places such as Madhu, Mihintale, and Vavuniya were avoided. The construction of the transmission line was strictly restrained to the ROW of the approved route; thus, no major deviations were considered. In 2013, prior to the project commencement, consultations with key stakeholders were held primarily to get their inputs and clearances for the Initial Environmental Examination report to be submitted to the Central Environment Authority. Consulted were key stakeholders such as District Secretary or Government Agent, Divisional Secretaries, Forest Department, Department of Wildlife (DOW), Irrigation Department, and Department of Archaeology (DOA), etc.

Securing land mine clearance was an issue in the section between Vavuniya and Anuradhapura. An international nongovernment organization was engaged to secure the clearance, but it was not supportive. Hence, the project sought the help of Sri Lanka Army who cleared around 80 mines. CEB then identified and labeled all the trees to be removed along the ROW of the transmission line, which was 35 meters to both sides from the center of the line. Permission was sought from the Forest Department and DOW to remove the trees. For security reasons, machinery had to be used for this purpose instead of manual labor. DOW initially objected to the use of heavy machinery, but later allowed it under strict conditions. The Forest Department allowed clearing only the trees within a 6-meter boundary and   only the removal of canopy/crown of the trees outside the 6-meter boundary, particularly in forest reservations and wildlife sanctuaries. CEB

paid compensation to the Forest Department for re-planting trees and for using timber jacks transported from Colombo to cut down the trees. Uprooting of trees belonging to the Forest Department was contracted to the Timber Corporation and its contractors in compliance with regulations. However, the contractors were not that enthusiastic to remove the trees inside a former war-torn area and to use light machinery as it was not very profitable to them. Therefore, CEB obtained permission to use its own manpower to remove the trees under the supervision of the Timber Corporation.

Construction work of the line was completed on 29 June 2019 and was energized in September 2019.

Raising Awareness on the Role of Divisional Secretaries

The transmission line traversed 10 DSDs. The initial awareness-raising program conducted for the 10 Divisional Secretaries explained the scope of the project, its ROW, technical details, and the type of civil works as well as the powers vested in the Divisional Secretaries as per the Electricity Act and its amendment. This awareness-raising program was useful in creating a complete understanding among the Divisional Secretaries who had to perform a major role in the project in granting clearance for the ROW as well as in handling grievances (Appendix 1). In this clearance certificate, the Divisional Secretary granted permission to install the transmission line subject to (i) payment of fair compensation for the trees to be removed on the ROW taking into consideration the life cycle of those trees, (ii) payment of compensation for the devaluation of land due to installation of transmission lines over such land, (iii) increase in the height of the conductors in places where they traverse houses and in areas of low elevation, and (iv) removal of only the essential trees to minimize adverse environmental impacts. Once the Divisional Secretaries granted clearance for the line routes, they also had the obligation to look into any objections raised by people over those line routes.

Relationship Building with Other Stakeholders

Apart from the initial awareness-raising program undertaken in 2013, continuous efforts were made by the project to build and strengthen rapport with other relevant stakeholders such as the Forest Department, DOW, Irrigation Department, DOA, Department of Agrarian Services (DAS), etc. through regular meetings and discussions, in order to get their support for the project implementation. The electrical superintendents and project engineers on-site played a strategic role in building and maintaining relationships with those stakeholders. This rapport was useful in getting timely clearance for the ROW of the transmission line. Appendix 2 presents a sample letter issued by the Irrigation Department giving its conditional clearance for the ROW to install the electricity lines.

Allowing Affected People to Raise Objections

The project ensured giving adequate time for people to raise their objections. In 2013, D Notice was issued to the households that would be affected by the project. The notice sought their permission for the wayleave clearance in terms of entry to the land for inspection and land surveying, removal of trees, excavation of pits, installation of towers and conductors, and repair and maintenance work. If the APs did not have objection, they were to notify the project manager of CEB within 21 days of receiving the notice. On the contrary, if they had any suggestions and/or proposals, they had to submit these to the Divisional Secretary, who is mandated to represent the Public Utilities Commission of Sri Lanka (PUCSL), and to the project manager. The D Notice further specified that the Divisional Secretary was empowered by PUCSL to accept and record any complaints from the public, to take appropriate action after organizing a hearing with those complainants, and to submit recommendations to the PUCSL. Moreover, if any preconditions were laid down by complainants in giving their consent for wayleave clearance and if such conditions were not acceptable to the project, such complaints were also to be forwarded to the Divisional Secretary for appropriate action (Appendix 3).

Types of Grievances/ Complaints and their Resolution

There were about 300 to 400 grievances and complaints from AP, mainly concerned about transmission lines traversing their land and houses, installation of towers on their land, and the loss of crops and trees. Some grievances and complaints and their remedial measures as reported by the APs are presented in Appendix 4.

*There were about 300 to 400 grievances and complaints from AP, mainly concerned about **transmission lines traversing their land and houses, installation of towers on their land, and the loss of crops and trees.***

Conducting a Hearing with the Complainants

The project received several complaints from APs since the transmission line began to affect their properties, trees, and paddy fields. Complaints were channeled to numerous agencies such as District Secretaries/Government Agents, Divisional Secretaries, CEB, and PUCSL. Some complaints were submitted to the President or the Prime Minister of Sri Lanka. When objections were raised, "objections clearance meetings" were conducted by the relevant Divisional Secretaries with the participation of both complainants and CEB to resolve those grievances.

In addition to the objections clearance meetings conducted by the Divisional Secretary, CEB project staff also participated in the grievance redress and problem-solving processes. For example, in one instance, a big group of war-displaced families, who were resettled in a site that fell within the

ROW earmarked for the transmission line, raised their objections as they wanted to build places of religious worship such as kovils and churches for their community. CEB organized a meeting with them with the participation of the secretary to the Ministry of Power and Energy and invited the priests, moulavis, and villagers to explain to them the national importance of the project, as well as the compensation scheme for the APs. Also, CEB conducted house-to-house visits to further raise their awareness specifically on the compensation that it offered which was higher than what that they were to get under involuntary land acquisition. As a result, majority of the complainants agreed to accept the compensation.

Assessment of Compensation

In the process of paying compensation, CEB encountered several issues and challenges. Many APs did not have any documentary evidence to support their land or tenurial rights. Some APs had lost the title deeds of their properties during

Partly constructed transmission tower in a property of a complainant (photo by OSPF).

the war while others who lived on government land did not have the government permits because they failed to renew these after the war. However, CEB ensured that they would be compensated for their losses whether they were titleholders or not.

Despite the fact that the Electricity Act had empowered the Divisional Secretaries to determine compensation, some of them wanted the Valuation Department to assess the losses and issue the valuation reports indicating the compensation to be paid to the APs. CEB, however, viewed this differently and did not encourage the Divisional Secretaries to depend on the Valuation Department since its assessments were comparatively lower and would not be acceptable to the APs. Instead, CEB encouraged the Divisional Secretaries to decide on compensation in compliance with the provisions in the Electricity Act.

In one instance, when a Divisional Secretary was reluctant to determine compensation by himself, the District Secretary appointed a committee to make a collective decision on fair compensation. This committee was composed of representatives from the Provincial Council, Land Ministry, Survey Department, DAS, etc. It recommended, that for land devaluation, to pay 50% of the market value, and for affected trees, to pay based on their market rates obtained from relevant institutions such as the Palmyrah Development Board, Coconut Development Board, Forest Department, etc. Compensation prescribed for a well-grown male Palmyrah tree was about SLR90,000, and for a coconut tree, it was SLR50,000. Appendix 5 shows a sample copy of the compensation assessed for affected trees of a household. People

were allowed to cut down their own trees and to retain the timber. Labor costs for this task was included in the tree values. Also, the Survey Department was advised not to exclude the ROW of the transmission line when surveying the land, so that the occupants or the people who occupied this land prior to the war would not lose their land rights and entitlements for compensation. Accordingly, the Divisional Secretary issued a letter to the APs confirming their entitlements to the ROW as well. Adequate vertical clearance was maintained to allow people to live within the ROW, and even to build 2-story houses. Livelihood assistance was recommended by the committee and cash assistance was given to construct agro-wells for the benefit of farmer communities. Compensation was paid for the loss of paddy and other crops. Land used for installation of transmission towers was also compensated at full market value. Land officers and Grama Niladharis of the DSD assisted in determining the compensation; hence, the need to get valuations from the Valuation Department did not arise.

Once the compensation was determined by the Divisional Secretary, CEB sends a payment voucher to the APs indicating their compensation entitlements. By signing this voucher, the APs signified their consent for wayleave clearance subject to receiving their compensation, and for the removal of the trees prior to receiving the compensation. Appendix 6 shows a sample copy of the payment voucher.

Thulhiriya-Kegalle 132-Kilovolt Transmission Line

Description

The 132 kV transmission line from Thulhiriya to Kegalle implemented by the CENEIP-P2 of CEB commenced its construction work in mid-2013 and was completed in August 2018. The line, with a total length of 22 km, traversed four DSDs—Warakapola, Kegalle, Rambukkana, and Galigamuwa—in the Kegalle district. This district located in the wet zone of Sri Lanka had an estimated population of 883,545 comprising 91% rural, 7% estate, and 2% urban. Population density is considerably high at 522 per square km. On the other hand, land occupancy is low, at 0.8 ha per household. The total cultivated area in the district is estimated at 82%, almost half of which is planted with major crops like tea, rubber, coconut, cinnamon, coffee, and pepper. Kegalle district claims 33% share of the rubber cultivation in Sri Lanka. Thus, land value in the district is significantly higher compared with those in the dry-zone districts.[10]

When the D Notice was issued, people raised objections to the transmission line. The objections were mainly from those who had built new houses on the land that they had bought from the original owners. These owners had sold out their land in the period between project design and implementation stages. The complaints were reported to the PUCSL, Divisional Secretaries, and CEB, with one complaining to ADB. There were around 40 grievances reported. The divisional secretary supported the grievance resolution process and, to minimize the impacts, suggested alterations to the original line route included in the initial environmental examination report and approved by the Central Environment Authority. Accordingly, the CEB altered the line route in two different sections which resulted in a deviation of the line length by 1,500 meters. The revised line route was able to reduce the number of affected houses by about seven. However, one of the APs whose property could not be avoided eventually sought legal action, and as a result, the project implementation was delayed by almost 1 year. Moreover, the project also suffered from contractor delays. Some cases as presented in Appendix 8 were based on the review of a sample of written complaints from the APs.

The project conducted awareness-raising programs for the four Divisional Secretaries on their role as detailed in the provisions in the Electricity Act. The District Secretary/Government Agent appointed a committee composed of the Divisional Secretary/Assistant Divisional Secretary, Grama Niladhari, technical officer of the divisional secretariat, and a project officer to determine compensation to the APs. Accordingly, the committee determined compensation for land devaluation whereas the Divisional Secretary determined compensation for affected trees.

---

[10] Department of Census and Statistics. 2018. District Statistical Handbook for Kegalle.

III. Grievance Redress Mechanism of the Electricity Project

None of the two transmission line projects had a project-based GRM. Instead, both used the existing government machinery as the main GRM for grievance resolution. In this context, the Divisional Secretary performed a central role in granting final clearance for the ROW of the transmission line, in receiving grievances and complaints from the APs, in hearing and resolving their objections and grievances, and in assessing compensation for the affected properties including trees and crops. The Sri Lanka Electricity Act (Amendment) No.31 of 2013 empowers the Divisional Secretary by delegating the powers, duties, and functions held by the PUCSL (Section 3 [b]) to authorize or prohibit installation of electricity lines on, over, or under any land; to inquire into the grievances reported by APs and to resolve such grievances; and to determine compensation to them affected people as stipulated in items 3, 4, 5, and 6 of Schedule 1 of Sri Lanka Electricity Act No. 20 of 2009. Complaints and grievances directed by APs to various agencies such as Grama Niladhari, CEB project offices, PUCSL, etc. had to be forwarded to the Divisional Secretary for his review, inquiry, and decision. In this grievance resolution process, the Divisional Secretary was assisted by the Grama Niladhari of the respective Grama Niladhari Division (GND) from where the complaint or the grievance had originated, and by other agencies such as DAS, Irrigation Department, Forest Department, Survey Department, DOA, Valuation Department, and CEB.

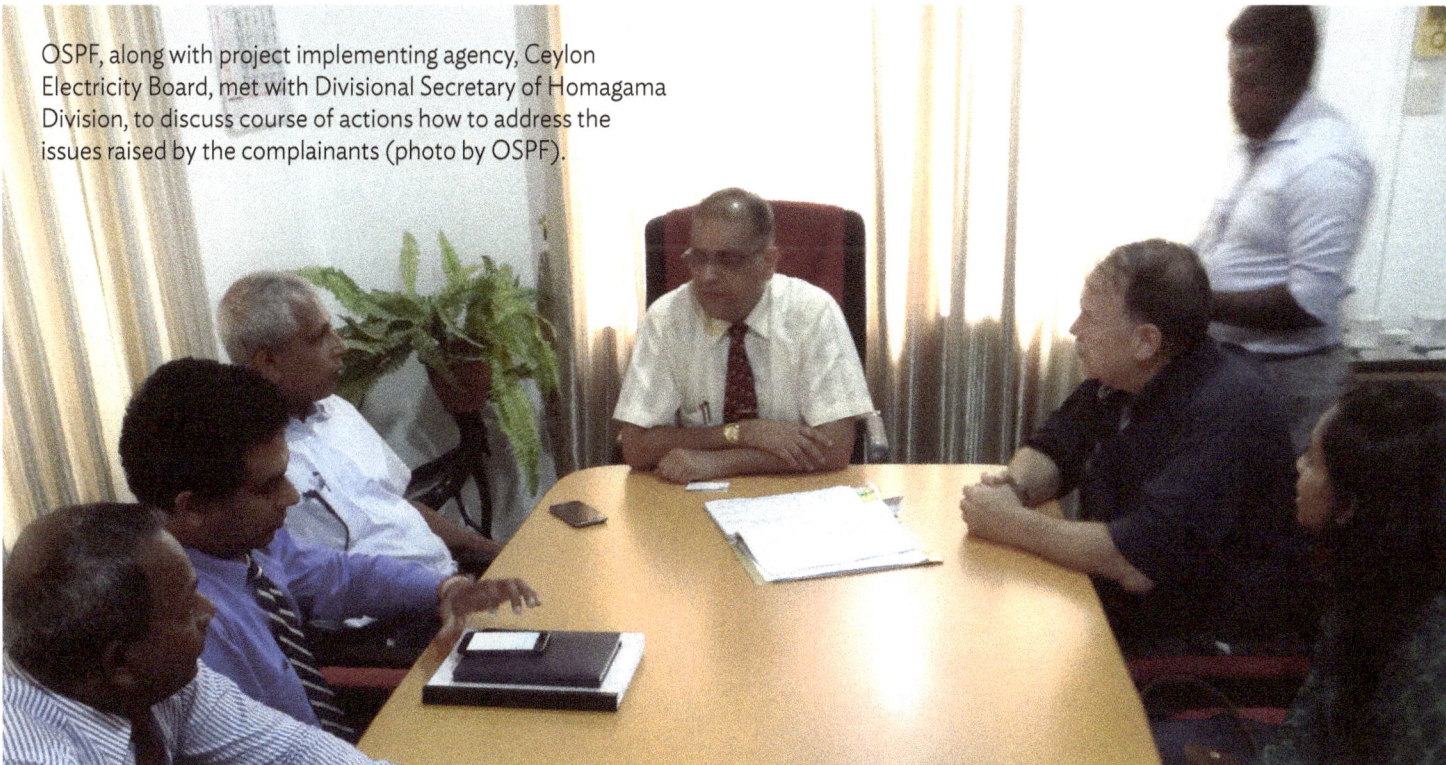

OSPF, along with project implementing agency, Ceylon Electricity Board, met with Divisional Secretary of Homagama Division, to discuss course of actions how to address the issues raised by the complainants (photo by OSPF).

IV. Lessons Learned

Site visit and consultations with complainants during the review and assessment of the complaint (photo by OSPF).

This section details some key features and lessons learned from the grievance redress and problem-solving experiences of the project.

- The two electricity projects used an existing administrative mechanism as their GRM in the process of grievance redress and problem solving. The GRM is empowered by the country's legal framework, the Sri Lanka Electricity Act.

- Consultations with communities and eliciting their views and suggestions, especially on the line route, and identifying the least impacted route were largely confined to the preliminary design stage of the project. However, the final route was determined based on the results of the ground surveys and technical and engineering requirements.

- The electricity projects did not involve any involuntary land acquisitions. However, cash compensation was provided to the APs for their losses such as land, crops, trees, and land devaluation. Conversely, APs in the electricity projects anticipated direct cash compensation for their losses. Determining such compensation entitlements had to be carried out within the country's legal framework and provisions, and by officers authorized for the purpose in order for such entitlements to be compliant with the country's financial regulations. A project-based GRM was not adequate in such situations. Therefore, the electricity projects were exclusively dependent on the Divisional Secretary who is empowered by the Sri Lanka Electricity Act to resolve reported grievances and determine compensation.

- Majority of the APs submitted their written complaints to the Divisional Secretaries while few others moved beyond the Divisional Secretary level and carried their grievances and complaints to higher levels of the administrative and political hierarchy. Meanwhile, some complaints were escalated to the country's judiciary. However, a few APs neither reported their grievances to the GRM nor participated in the grievance resolution process either because they did not have the capacity and the knowledge to frame their grievances or because they had personal concerns such as their health or the absence of any other family member to accompany them for inquiries, etc. Despite this, the project followed the general procedures that applied to all the APs, assessed the losses of these vulnerable households, and provided them with fair compensation despite their non participation in the formal grievance redress process. An important lesson for development projects is to ensure that vulnerable households are assisted in the process of their displacements, as well as in the grievance resolution process, and that they are extended fair compensation to cover their losses.

The two electricity projects used an existing administrative mechanism as their GRM in the process of grievance redress and problem solving. The GRM is empowered by the country's legal framework, the Sri Lanka Electricity Act.

Neither a project-based GRM nor a legally instituted GRM can resolve the grievances resulting from CENEIP in isolation. Both require additional support from other concerned stakeholders to address the grievances. This complementary role was efficiently performed by the field-level project staff who significantly contributed to reduce the number of grievances and complaints that would have been otherwise reported to the formal GRM.

Grievance resolution is not a one-off activity. As the case pointed out, it requires several rounds of discussion and negotiations, compromise between concerned parties, and reaching agreements to share resources and contribute to the problem-solving process.

OSPF conducted consultations with complainants and other affected people as part of its review and assessment process to determine whether and under what conditions a problem-solving process should proceed (photo by OSPF).

Appendixes

1. Line Route Clearance Certificate from Divisional Secretary

Divisional Secretariat, Nuwaragam Palatha East Anuradhapura

18.2.2016

The Project Manager
Mannar Transmission Infrastructure Development Project
No. 35.2, Ground Floor, Park Road
Mabole, Wattala

Clean Energy and Network Efficiency Improvement Project – Package 1 - Mannar Transmission Infrastructure Development Project – Lot B

Reference your letter dated 29.1.2016 on the above subject.

I, hereby give my permission for the proposed transmission line route which would pass through the existing 33 kV medium voltage distribution line route alongside the paddy fields and the Kirikkulama tank, subject to the payment of fair compensation for the trees to be removed within the right-of-way of the transmission line, taking into account the life-cycle value of the trees, payment of compensation for land devaluation due to transmission line traversing such land after an assessment of the land value, raising the height of the transmission line in places where it crosses over houses and in areas of low elevation, and removal of only the essential trees to minimize adverse environmental impacts.

Signed:

W.M.Ruwan Wijesinghe
Divisional Secretary
Divisional Secretariat,
Muwaragam Palatha East,
Anuradhapura

ප්‍රාදේශීය මහලේකම් කාර්යාලය
නැගෙනහිර නුවරගම් පළාත අනුරාධපුරය
பிரதேச செயலகம்
கிழக்கு நுவரகம் பிராந்தியம் - அனுராதபுரம்
Divisional Secretariat
Nuwaragam Palatha East Anuradhapura

මගේ අංකය :අනු/8/5/6/විදුලි ව්‍යාපෘති/මන්නාරම

එවනු ඔබේ ඔබේ අංකයපිටපත/පිරිත්තේ්වුඔුම- 81/මම/20(A)

උ.ඟ.තු ඔබේ

දිනය

තික 2016.02.18

ව්‍යාපෘති කළමණාකරු,
මන්නාරම සම්ප්‍රේෂණ යටිතල පහසුකම් ව්‍යාපෘතිය,
අංක 35/2, පළමු මහල, උද්‍යාන පාර,
මාබෝල, වත්තල.

පිවිතුරු බලශක්ති ජාලගත කාර්යක්ෂමතා වැඩිදියුණු කිරීමේ ව්‍යාපෘතිය - 01 පැකේජය
මන්නාරම සම්ප්‍රේෂණ යටිතල පහසුකම් - ලොට් බි.

උක්ත කරුණ සම්බන්ධයෙන් ඔබගේ සමාංක හා 2016.01.29 දිනැති ලිපිය හා බැදේ.

02.   ඒ අනුව විදුලි රැහැන් මග ඉදි කිරීමට යෝජිත කහවගස්දිගිලිය චෝට් 33,000 රැහැන් මග ඔස්සේම චෙල් යාය හා කිරික්කුලම වැව ආසන්නයේ නව අනුරාධපුර ග්‍රීඩ් උප පොල දක්වා මෙම විදුලි රැහැන් මාර්ගය ගමන් කිරීමේදී, ගමන් මාර්ගයේ ඇති ඉවත් කිරීමට සිදුවන ගස්වල ජීවිත කාලය සලකා සාධාරණ වන්දි මුදලක් ගෙවීමටත්, විදුලි මාර්ගය ගමන් කරන ඉඩම් වල අඩුවන වටිනාකම තක්සේරු කර ගෙවීමටත්, නිවාස මතින් විදුලි මාර්ගය ගමන් කිරීමේදී හා බෑවුම් සහිත ස්ථාන වලදී විදුලි මාර්ගය උස්කර ඉදිකිරීමටත්, මෙහිදී පරිසර හානි අවම වනසේ අත්‍යාවශ්‍යා ගස් පමණක් ඉවත් කිරීමට ද යටත්ව මෙම සම්ප්‍රේෂණ මාර්ගය සඳහා මාර්ග අවසරය ලබා දෙනබව කාරුණිකව දන්වමි.

ඩබ්.එම්. රුවන් විජේසිංහ
ප්‍රාදේශීය ලේකම්
නැගෙනහිර නුවරගම් පළාත,
අනුරාධපුර.

ඩබ්.එම් රුවන් විජේසිංහ,
ප්‍රාදේශීය ලේකම්,
ප්‍රාදේශීය ලේකම් කාර්යාලය,
නැගෙනහිර නුවරගම් පළාත,
අනුරාධපුර.

2. Line Route Clearance Certificate from Provincial Irrigation Department

15.6.2016

Eng. W.F.M. Fernando
Project Manager
Ceylon Electricity Board

Clean Energy and Network Efficiency Improvement Project – Package 1 - Mannar Transmission Infrastructure Development Project – Lot B

Reference your letter No.PM/CENEIP-P1/TE/30 dated 2.6.2016.

I hereby inform you that we have no objection to the construction of the transmission line within the proposed route subject to the conditions specified in the second paragraph of your letter.

Signed:

Eng. H.M.J. Herath
Provincial Director of Irrigation
Provincial Irrigation Department
North Central Province

මாகாண நீர்ப்பாசனத் திணைக்களம்
வட மத்திய மாகாணம்

PROVINCIAL IRRIGATION DEPARTMENT
NORTH CENTRAL PROVINCE

මෛත්‍රීපාල සේනානායක මාවත, අනුරාධපුරය.
மைத்திரிபால சேனாநாயக்க மாவத்தை, அநுராதபுரம்.
Maithripala Senanayake Mawatha, Anuradhapura.

මගේ අංකය எனது இல. My No.	NCP/PID/ED19/ඉරුම්පොදු/2016	ඔබේ අංකය உமது இல. Your No.		දිනය திகதி Date	2016.06.15 2016.07.15

ඉංජිනේරු

ඩබ්ලිව්.එල්.එම්.ප්‍රනාන්දු

ව්‍යාපෘති කළමනාකරු

ලංකා විදුලිබල මණ්ඩලය

පිවිතුරු බලශක්ති ජාලගත කාර්යක්ෂමතා වැඩිදියුණු කිරීමේ ව්‍යාපෘතිය-01 පැකේජය මන්නාරම

සමෝධාන යටිතල පහසුකම් –ලොට් බී

උක්ත කරුණට අදාළව ඔබගේ අංක පිඑම්/සිඊඑන්ටීඅයි-ඒ1/ටීඊ/30 හා 2016.06.02 දිනැති ලිපිය හා බැඳේ.

02. ඒ අනුව ඔබ විසින් එවන ලද ලිපියේ දෙවන ඡේදයේ සඳහන් කොන්දේසි වලට යටත්ව රැහැන් මාර්ගය ඉදිකිරීම පිළිබඳව අපගේ විරුද්ධත්වයක් නොමැති බව කාරුණිකව දන්වා සිටිමි.

පළාත් වාරිමාර්ග අධ්‍යක්ෂ.

පළාත්වාරිමාර්ග දෙපාර්තමේන්තුව,

උතුරු මැද පළාත.

ඉංජි.වයි.එම්.ජේ. හේරත්
පළාත් වාරිමාර්ග අධ්‍යක්ෂ
පළාත් වාරිමාර්ග දෙපාර්තමේන්තුව
උතුරු මැද පළාත

වාරිමාර්ග අධ්‍යක්ෂ நீர்ப்பாசன பணிப்பாளர் Irrigation Director	} 025-2237569	යෝජනා අංශය திட்டமிடல் பிரிவு Planning Section	} 025-3779061	ෆැක්ස් අංකය தொ.நகல் நகல் Fax No.	} 025-2234767
කාර්යාලය அலுவலகம் Office	} 025-2234767	ගිණුම් අංශය கணக்குப் பிரிவு Account Section	} 025-2237586	ඊ-මේල් மின் அஞ்சல் E-mail	} ncpirrigation@gmail.com

3. D Notice Requesting Permissions for Wayleave Clearance

My No: CENEIP-P1/TE 20/D – 490

23.2.2015

Mannar Transmission Infrastructure Development Project
Ceylon Electricity Board,
39/1, Kalaeliya Road, Kapuwatte
Ja-Ela

Notice requesting permission for wayleave clearance – Proposed Anuradhapura-Vavunia-Mannar 220 kV Transmission Line

Notice issued to Mr. S.J. Anil Jayaweera to obtain permission for wayleave clearance in the land referred to below in terms of the item 3 (1) (a) of Schedule 1 of the Sri Lanka Electricity Act No.20 of 2009.

Address of the land: No.11, Ulpathgama, Medawachchiya
Divisional Secretariat Division: Medawachchiya
Grama Niladhari Division: Thulana No.60, Kanadaradivulwewa

Permission for wayleave clearance (footnote 1) is required for the following:
(1) Felling the trees;
(2) Excavation of pits;
(3) Installation of towers;
(4) Installation of conductors;
(5) Entry to the land for surveying and inspections

If you agree to grant permission for the above, please inform the Project Manager whose address is given below within 21 days of receiving this Notice. If you failed to notify within 21 days, it will be considered your no objection to our proposal, and steps will be taken to implement the proposed action plan.

If you have any alternative proposals, please forward them to the relevant Divisional Secretary (who represents the Public Utilities Commission of Sri Lanka) whose administrative area under which the above mentioned land is located with a copy to the Project Manager. The address of the Project Manager is given below.

Please note that the Divisional Secretaries are empowered to receive public complaints, register the written complaints, give fair hearing to the complainants, and take appropriate measures on behalf of the Public Utilities Commission, and to submit his/her recommendations to the Public Utilities Commission.

If the conditions and suggestions that you submit within 21 days of receiving this Notice are not acceptable to us, they will be forwarded to the Divisional Secretary to take appropriate action.

Also, if you require any further clarifications, please write to the Project Manager whose address is given below.

Signed:

Authorized officer of the licensee

Name of the authorized officer: Project Manager

Address: Mannar Transmission Infrastructure Development Project,
Ceylon Electricity Board,
39/1, Kalaeliya Road,
Kapuwatte, Ja-Ela

Telephone: 011-3168771 / 2240099 Fax: 011- 2240860

මන්නාරම සම්ප්‍රේෂණ යටිතල පහසුකම් ව්‍යාපෘතිය, ලංකා විදුලිබල මණ්ඩලය
39/1, කලඋලිය පාර, කපුවත්ත, ජා-ඇල.

මාර්ග අවසරය ඉල්ලා සිටීමේ නිවේදනය
යෝජිත අනුරාධපුර - වව්නියා - මන්නාරම ද.වෝ. 220 විදුලි රැහැන

....වෙත

2009 අංක 20 දරණ ශ්‍රී ලංකා විදුලිබල පනතේ 1 වන උපලේඛනයේ අයිතම 3 (1) (ආ) අනුව පහත ස්ථානයේ පිහිටි ඉඩම සඳහා අවශ්‍ය මාර්ග අවසරය ලබාදීම සම්බන්ධයෙන් කරනු ලබන දැනුම්දීමයි.

ඉඩමේ ලිපිනය : ....

....

ප්‍රාදේශීය ලේකම් කොට්ඨාසය : ....

ග්‍රාමනිලධාරී කොට්ඨාසය : ....

අවශ්‍ය මාර්ග අවසරය* පිළිබඳ විස්තරය පහත දැක්වේ.

1. ගල් කැපීම   4. සමීඛ ඇදීම
2. වළවල් හෑරීම   5. මැනීම හා නිරීක්ෂණ කටයුතු සඳහා ඇතුළුවීම
3. කුණුණු සිටුවීම

ඉඩය සඳහන් මාර්ග අවසරය ලබා දීමට ඔබ එකඟ වන්නේ නම්, කරුණාකර මෙම දැන්වීම ලැබී දින 21 ක් තුළ පහත ලිපිනය දරණ ව්‍යාපෘති කළමණාකරු වෙත දන්වන්න. මෙම දැන්වීම ලැබී දින 21 ක් තුළ දැනුම්දීමට අපොහොසත් වුවහොත් අපගේ යෝජනාවට විරුද්ධත්වයක් නැති බව තීරණය කර යෝජිත වැඩ පිළිවෙළ ක්‍රියාත්මක කිරීමට කටයුතු කරනු ලැබේ.

මේ සම්බන්ධව ඔබට වෙනත් යෝජනා ඉදිරිපත් කිරීමට ඇත්නම්, කරුණාකර එය මහජන උපයෝගිතා කොමිෂන් සභාව නියෝජනය කරන ඉඩය සඳහන් ඉඩම අයත් ප්‍රදේශයේ ප්‍රාදේශීය ලේකම් වෙත ද එහි පිටපතක් පහත ලිපිනය දරණ ව්‍යාපෘති කළමණාකරු වෙත යොමු කිරීමට කටයුතු කරන්න.

මහජන උපයෝගිතා කොමිෂන් වෙනුවෙන් මහජන සැමිණිලි ලබා ගැනීමට ලිඛිත විරෝධතා පවත්පත් කර ගැනීමට සහ සාධාරණ සවන්දීමකින් අනතුරුව සුදුසු ක්‍රියාමාර්ග ගැනීමටත් මහජන උපයෝගිතා කොමිෂන් වෙත නිර්දේශ ඉදිරිපත් කිරීමටත් ප්‍රාදේශීය ලේකම්වරුන් වෙත බලය පවරා ඇති බව කරුණාවෙන් සලකන්න.

මෙම දැන්වීම ලැබී දින 21 ක් තුළ ඉදිරිපත් කරන මාර්ග අවසරය පිළිබඳව ඔබගේ කොන්දේසි හා නියමයන් අප හට පිළිගැනීමට නොහැකි නම් ඒ සඳහා සුදුසු ක්‍රියාමාර්ගයක් ගැනීමට අදාළ ප්‍රාදේශීය ලේකම්වරුන් වෙත යොමු කරනු ඇත.

එසේම මේ සම්බන්ධ පවදුරටත් සැහැදිලි සිටීමක් අවශ්‍ය නම් කරුණාකර පහත ලිපිනය දරණ ව්‍යාපෘති කළමණාකරු අමතන මෙන් කාරුණිකව දන්වමි.

....
(බලපත්‍රලාභියාගේ බලයලත් නිලධාරී)

බලයලත් නිලධාරීයාගේ නම : ව්‍යාපෘති කළමණාකරු

ලිපිනය   : මන්නාරම සම්ප්‍රේෂණ යටිතල පහසුකම් ව්‍යාපෘතිය, ලංකා විදුලිබල මණ්ඩලය,

                                         39/1, කලඋලිය පාර, කපුවත්ත, ජා-ඇල.

දුරකථන අංකය   : 011-3168771/ 2240099   ෆැක්ස්: 011-2240860

*"අවශ්‍ය මාර්ග අවසරය" ගන්නේ ඉඩම මත, යට හෝ උඩින් විදුලි රැහැන් සවි කිරීම පිණිස සවිකොට පැමීම පිණිස බලපත්‍රලාභිය දෙනු ලබන කැමැත්ත සහ විදුලි රැහැන පරීක්ෂා කිරීමේ, නඩත්තු කිරීමේ, ගැලවීමේ, අලුත්වැඩියා කිරීමේ, වෙනස් කිරීමේ, ප්‍රතියෝජනය කිරීමේ හෝ ඉවත් කිරීමේ කාර්ය සඳහා ඉඩමට ප්‍රවේශය පිණිස ඉදිරිම අදහස් වේ.

4. Anuradhapura–Mannar 220-Kilovolt Transmission Line Cases

This section presents a few grievances/complaints and their remedial measures as reported by persons affected by the transmission line.

Case No. 1: The affected person (AP) is a settler and occupied 3 acres of government land obtained under a permit. The project caused her loss of 15 coconut trees, 4 jackfruit trees, 3 mango trees, 7 teak trees, and some other timber trees. She opposed the removal of trees and complained to the Divisional Secretary, who in turn, requested the Ceylon Electricity Board (CEB) to inquire into her grievances. Thereafter, the Divisional Secretary invited her to his office and heard her grievances. Despite her living on government land, the Divisional Secretary considered her land ownership and entitlements for compensation as she proved her tenurial rights by producing her electricity bills. In the end, the AP agreed to accept compensation for her affected trees which amounted to SLR465,000, and to cut the trees. She used part of her compensation and timber for her house construction and shared the balance with her daughter who lives in the adjoining land.

Case No. 2 (interview given by AP's daughter): The transmission line traversed the AP's land and close to her house which resulted in the removal of 11 coconut trees, 3 mango trees, and several banana clumps. She complained to the Divisional Secretary, objecting to the removal of trees, and expressed concerns over the family safety. Since the line crossed over a substantial part of her land, she would not be able to plant any tall trees in future. After her inquiry with the Divisional Secretary, the AP agreed to accept the compensation which also included additional compensation for line traversing very close to her house. The compensation she received amounted to SLR220,000, part of which she spent to cover the funeral expenses of her husband who died during the same period. The AP presently lives and works in a Middle East country.

Case No. 3: The AP, together with his neighborhood, objected to the line traversing their land. They later consented to the project after assurances given by the Divisional Secretary to pay compensation for their affected assets. One transmission tower was installed on his land, and moreover, he lost 10 palmyrah trees, a mango tree, and a timber tree. The AP received SLR123,000 for the land lost for the tower base, and another SLR132,000 for the affected trees. Meanwhile, during civil works of the project, the crops cultivated by the AP in an area of about one-fourth acre of land were damaged. He complained to the CEB as well as to the Public Utilities Commission of Sri Lanka. CEB requested him to obtain an assessment of his crop losses from the Department of Agrarian Services, which estimated a compensation of SLR94,500. CEB paid the compensation and the AP was satisfied.

Case No. 4: The AP lives on a land obtained under a government permit. She permanently lost part of her paddy land for three legs of a transmission tower installed on her land. She complained to the Divisional Secretary and objected to the tower installation. However, the Divisional Secretary persuaded her to allow the tower installation and assured compensation. Since the tower had been erected on a paddy land, the compensation assessment was lower than that paid for highlands. The AP received SLR27,500. However, she is unhappy about what she felt was the discriminatory compensation for paddy and highlands. She would no longer be able to cultivate the land under the tower as there was a concrete layer underneath the footing areas, and also, she would already be unable to use tractors inside the tower base area. She also lost two palmyrah trees, one tamarind tree, six margosa trees, and several other timber trees. Meanwhile, she had been deceived by a man who cultivated the nearby land by covertly taking the compensation paid for trees without her knowledge. She complained to the Grama Niladhari who intervened to recover the lost compensation which amounted to SLR25,000. The AP shared part of the compensation with her six children and used the balance on pilgrimages.

Case No. 5: The transmission line traversed very close to the AP's house, resulting in the loss of about 35 coconut trees, of which 10-15 were bearing fruits at the time of their removal. She also lost several other timber trees including 3-4 margosa trees. She neither complained to the Divisional Secretary nor participated in the inquiries conducted due to her ill-health and the fact that she lived alone. The Grama Niladhari assessed her losses, and the Divisional Secretary determined the compensation, which was SLR341,000 including the additional compensation for the impacts of the line that traversed close to her house. Though she was unhappy with the compensation that she received for the coconut trees, she used her compensation to build two rooms her house. .

Case No. 6: The AP lived with her husband on a one-half acre land obtained on government permits. The transmission line caused the loss of a mango tree, a coconut tree, five palmyrah trees, and a few other timber trees. The AP complained to the Divisional Secretary but did not participate in the inquiries. She received SLR80,000 for the affected trees which she used for her house improvements. Further, during the civil works, the heavy machinery used damaged her cultivation field for which no compensation had been paid. She used her own money to restore the land. She intended planting trees on the remaining portion of the land.

Case No. 7: The transmission line traversed the land of the AP, resulting in the loss of two palmyrah trees, two margosa trees, and five other timber trees grown around his paddy field. . However, the AP did not raise any objections. He received SLR70,000 as compensation for the loss of trees, and he was satisfied with what he received.

Case No. 8: The AP is the daughter of the title holder. She lost 17 coconut trees, a mango tree, a jackfruit tree, and a timber tree (thelembu tree) which was dedicated to a pulleyar god. In addition, two legs of a transmission tower was installed in a part of her paddy field. With this, she could no longer cultivate underneath the tower. The AP never complained to the Divisional Secretary since she thought that it was not proper to complain about a government project. She received SLR311,000 for the affected trees, and another SLR24,800 for the land lost for tower foundation.

Case No. 9: The AP is unmarried living with her unmarried brother. She ran a pre-school, while her brother is engaged in agriculture. The AP owned about 3 acres of land, but titles are available for only 1 acre. CEB insisted that the AP should be paid compensation irrespective of her titles. She lost 50-60 timber trees though these did not have much commercial value. A transmission tower was also installed on her land for which she received SLR60,000. She also received SLR140,000 for the lost. She used part of the compensation to have electricity in her house.

Case No. 10: The AP lost 18 coconut trees, 5 jackfruit trees, 3 margosa trees and several other fruit-bearing and non-fruit bearing trees. Though he did not complain to the Divisional Secretary, his losses were assessed and he was compensated the amount of SLR735,000. The AP used part of the money to repair his house, and the balance was deposited in the bank. He now cultivates small size crops such as banana and lime under the conductor.

5. Compensation Estimates for Affected Trees within the Right of Way

Name of the Grama Niladhari: D M W D Dissanayake	Ceylon Electricity Board	My No.
Registered No: No.59	Proposed Anuradhapura– Vavunia– Mannar 220 kV Transmission Line	Name of the Divisional Secretary:
Division: Akirikanda		Divisional Secretary's Division: Medawachchiya
		District Secretary's Division:
		Province:

Felling and removal of trees should be carried out only by landowners

Land lot No.	Angle tower No.	Name of the land	Name of the owners and addresses	No. trees to be removed	Details of trees/ground damages/crop damages	Unit rate (SLRs)	Total amount (SLRs)	Voucher No.	Date voucher was posted to the owner	Date of receiving the voucher from the owner	Date of submitting the voucher to electrical superintendent	Date of receiving the voucher from the Electrical Superintendent	Date of submitting to the Accountant	Any other details
107	AP 12	Highland	A S Jayasiri Karapikkada Medawachchiya	4	Hik 1'	500	2,000							
				3	Hoorimara 1.5'	1,750	5,250							
				1	Hoorimara 1'	1,000	1,000							
				2	Hoorimara 3'	5,500	1,100							
				2	Hoorimara 2'	4,000	8,000							
				1	Burutha 1'	2,000	2,000							
				4	Maila 1'	1,000	4,000							
				1	Hoorimara 4.5'	7,500	7,500							
				1	Koon 7.5'	7,250	7,250							
				1	Kaduru 1.5'	750	750							
				6	Kaduru 1"	500	3,000							
							51,750							

Proposed Anuradhapura - Vavuniya - Mannar 220 kV Transmission Line Route

ඉඩම් අංකය	කණු කර්මාන්ත අංකය	ඉඩම් හිමි නම	අයිතිකරුවන්ගේ නම හා ලිපිනය	කැපිය යුතු ගස් ගණන	කැපිය යුතු පැළවල විස්තරය	අගනු ප්‍රමාණය එකක් රු./ග	මිල ප්‍රමාණය රු./ග		එකඟ අංකය						වෙනත් කරුණු
107	AP 12	මෙම ඉඩම	ඒ.ජේ.ජයසිරි මයා	04	කොස් 1'	500 00	2,000 00		ANVA/HE/	16/11/16	10/07/14	10/07/14	14/07/17		
			කඹුරුගම, මඩවච්චිය	03	පුවක් ගස 1.5'	1,750 00	5,250 00		AKR/109						
				01	පුවක් ගස 1'	1,000 00	1,000 00								
				02	පුවක් ගස 3'	5,500 00	11,000 00								
				02	පුවක් ගස 2'	4,000 00	8,000 00								
				01	ඉඳිආ 1'	2,000 00	2,000 00								
				04	කෝපි 1'	1,000 00	4,000 00								
				01	පුවක් ගස 4.5'	7,500 00	7,500 00								
				01	කෙසෙල් 7.5'	7,250 00	7,250 00								
				01	තොරුම් 1.5'	750 00	750 00								
				06	තොරුම් 1'	500 00	3,000 00								
					සම්පූර්ණ නිෂ්පාදිතයේ සමස්ත පාඩුව රුපි.		51,750 00		PB NO: 980-51/PEA/19/0377	18/07/2017					

6. Compensation Payment Voucher

CEYLON ELECTRICITY BOARD

Your No: My No: PM/CENEIP/P1/TE/20 (D)   16th November 2016

Mr. A S Jayasiri
Karapikkada
Medawachchiya

Proposed Anuradhapura-Vavunia-Mannar 220kV
Transmission Line

Clean Energy and Network Efficiency
Improvement Project - Package 1
(Mannar Transmission Infrastructure Development Project)

Voucher No.	ANVA/ME/AKR/107
Approved compensation	SLR 51,750
Assessment reference	AN/3/3/1/1/34-i
Divisional Secretary's Division	Medawachchiya
Grama Niladhari Division where land/cultivated land is located	Akirikanda
Name of the village where land/cultivated land is located	Karapikkada

Payment of compensation for land/cultivation fields

The appended payment voucher indicates the amount of compensation estimated by the Divisional Secretary, Mr. D.M. Shantha Bandara in terms of the provisions in Schedule 1 (Amended) of Sri Lanka Electricity Act No.20 of 2009 for the above mentioned land/cultivated land affected by the construction of the transmission line from Anuuradhapura to Mannar under the Mannar Transmission Infrastructure Development Project.

Also, we kindly request you to cut down and remove all trees which are marked with the symbol 'E' and included for the assessment of compensation within a period of two weeks. Since the cost of cutting and removing the trees is also included in the compensation, it is required that you remove the trees prior to the payment of compensation. (Note: Removal of some trees and their transportation requires a permit. Please obtain necessary information from the Grama Niladhari).

Please sign and return the appended payment voucher together with the letter that indicates your bank account number/s in order to proceed with the payment of compensation. If the amount of compensation recommended for you is SLR25,000 or above, your signature on the payment voucher should be placed on a stamp with a value of SLR25/-. If the compensation amount is less than SLR25,000, your signature can be placed on the appropriate place without a stamp. If there was an error in the name entered in the payment voucher, please enclose a letter indicating the correct name certified by the Grama Niladhari/Vice Chairman along with the completed payment voucher. If the thumb mark was placed instead of signature, it should be attested by the Grama Niladhari or the Divisional Secretary.

Please enclose the following documents required for the payment of compensation.
1.   A copy of the land title/deed or the permit
2.   Permission granted for wayleave clearance
3.   Photocopy of the National Identity Card

4. Payment voucher
5. Details of your bank account/s
6. A copy of the bank account book/s

We appreciate your cooperation for the successful implementation of this project which is of high national importance.

Thank you,

Yours faithfully,

Project Manager, CENEIP – P1
Mannar Transmission Infrastructure Development Project
Ceylon Electricity Board

ලංකා විදුලිබල මණ්ඩලය
இலங்கை மின்சார சபை
CEYLON ELECTRICITY BOARD

ඔබගේ අංකය:	මගේ අංකය: පිඑම්/සිර්ඔත්ර්අයිපි-81/පිපි/20(D)	දිනය: 2016 නොවැම්බර් මස 16 වැනිදා

ඒ.එස්. ජයසිරි මයා
කරවික්කඩ,
මැදවච්චිය.

වවුචර් අංකය	**ANVA/ME/AKR/107**
නිර්දේශිත වන්දි මුදල	රු. 51,750.00
තක්සේරු යොමුව	අනු/3/3/1/1/34-i
ප්‍රාදේශීය ලේකම් කොට්ඨාශය	මැදවච්චිය
ඉඩම්/ වගා කිම පිහිටි ග්‍රාම නිලධාරී කොට්ඨාශය	ඈසිපිකඋන්ද
ඉඩම්/ වගා කිම පිහිටි ග්‍රාමයේ නාමය	කරවික්කඩ

යෝජිත අනුරාධපුර - වවිනියාව - මන්නාරම ද.වෝ 220 විදුලි
සම්ප්‍රේෂණ මාර්ගය
පිවිතුරු බලශක්ති ජාලගත කාර්යක්ෂමතා වැඩිදියුණු කිරීමේ
ව්‍යාපෘතිය - 01 ඇලක්ෂය
(මන්නාරම සම්ප්‍රේෂණ යටිතල පහසුකම්)

ඉඩම්/ වගාබිම් සඳහා වන්දි ගෙවීම

මන්නාරම සම්ප්‍රේෂණ යටිතල පහසුකම් ව්‍යාපෘතිය යටතේ අනුරාධපුරය සිට මන්නාරම දක්වා වූ විදුලි සම්ප්‍රේෂණ මාර්ගය ඉදිකිරීමේදී ඉහත දක්වා ඇති ඉඩමට / වගාබිමට සිදු වූ / සිදුවන අලාභය වෙනුවෙන් 2009 අංක 20 දරණ ශ්‍රී ලංකා විදුලිබල පනතේ 01 වන උපලේඛනය (සංශෝධිත) අනුව ප්‍රාදේශීය ලේකම් ඩි.එම්. ශාන්ත දසනායක මහතා විසින් තක්සේරු කර ඇති මුදල මේ සමග එවා ඇති ගෙවුම් වවුචරයේ දක්වා ඇත.

තවද, ලදසතියක් ඇතුළත "E" අක්ෂරය යොදා සලකුණු කර ඇති සහ වන්දි තක්සේරුවට ඇතුළත් කර ඇති ගස් සියල්ල කපා ඉවත් කර ගන්නා මෙන් කාරුණිකව දන්වමු. ගස් කපා ඉවත් කිරීමේ ගාස්තුවද මෙම තක්සේරුවට ඇතුළත් කර ඇති හෙයින්, වන්දි මුදල් ගෙවීමට පෙර එම ගස් ඔබ විසින් කපා ඉවත් කල යුතු වේ. (සටහන: සමහර දැව වර්ග කපා ඉවත් කිරීමට/ ප්‍රවාහනයට බලපත්‍ර ලබා ගැනීමට අවශ්‍ය වේ. වැඩි විස්තර ප්‍රදේශයේ ග්‍රාම නිලධාරී මහතාගෙන් ලබා ගන්න.)

වන්දි ගෙවීම සඳහා, මේ සමග එවා ඇති ගෙවීම් වවුචරය සහ ඔබගේ ශිෂ්‍යම අංක දැක්වෙන ලිපිය සම්පූර්ණ කර අප වෙත එවන්න. ගෙවීම් වවුචරය අත්සන් තැබීමේදී, නිර්දේශික වන්දි මුදල රු. 25,000.00 ඒ ට ව වැඩි නම් රු. 25.00 ක වටිනාකමකින් යුත් මුද්දරයක් අලවා ඒ මත අත්සන් තැබීමට අමතක නොකරන්න. නිර්දේශික වන්දි මුදල රු. 25,000.00 ව අඩු නම් මුද්දරය නොමැතිව අදාල ස්ථානයේ අත්සන් තබන්න. ගෙවීම් වවුචරයෙහි සඳහන් නම වැරදි නම් ග්‍රාම නිලධාරී හා ප්‍රාදේශීය ලේකම්/ උප සභාපති කුමා විසින් සහතික කරන ලද ලිපියක් සමග වවුචරය සම්පූර්ණ කර මා වෙත එවිය යුතුය. ඇඟිලි සලකුණු තැබුවහොත් එය ග්‍රාම නිලධාරී හා ප්‍රාදේශීය ලේකම් මගින් සහතික කර ගත යුතුය.

තක්සේරු කර ඇති වන්දි මුදල් ලබා දීම සඳහා පහත දක්වා ඇති ලිපි ලේඛනද අප වෙත එවන්න.

1. ඉඩමේ ඔප්පු පිටපත හෝ බලපතුයේ පිටපතක්
2. මාර්ග අවසරය ලබා දීමේ ලිපිය
3. ජාතික හැඳුනුම්පතේ ජායා පිටපතක්
4. ගෙවීම් වවුචරය
5. බැංකු ගිණුම් විස්තරය
6. බැංකු ගිණුම් පොතේ පිටපතක්

ජාතික වශයෙන් ඉතා ඉහල වැදගත්කමක් ඇති මෙම ව්‍යාපෘතියේ ඉදිකිරීම් කටයුතු සාර්ථකව කරගෙන යාම සඳහා ඔබගෙන් ලැබෙන සහයෝගය අපි ඉතා අගය කොට සලකමු.

ස්තූතියි,
මෙයට විශ්වාසී වූ,

ව්‍යාපෘති කළමණාකරු - සිර්ඇන්ඩ්ඔත්ර්අයිපි-81
(මන්නාරම සම්ප්‍රේෂණ යටිතල පහසුකම් ව්‍යාපෘතිය)
ලංකා විදුලිබල මණ්ඩලය

සිර්ඔත්ර්අයිපි-81: මන්නාරම සම්ප්‍රේෂණ යටිතල පහසුකම් ව්‍යාපෘති කාර්යාලය
35/2, පළමු මහල, උදයත පාර, මාබෝල, වත්තල, ශ්‍රී ලංකාව.
දු.ක: +94 11 3168771 / 2936488 / ෆැක්ස්: +94 11 4544564 | විද්‍යුත් ලිපිනය: pmceneip@ceb.lk

Project Manager, CENEIP - P1
(Mannar Transmission Infrastructure Development Project)
Ceylon Electricity Board
35/2, First Floor, Park Road,
Mabole, Wattala

Voucher No.	ANVA/ME/AKR/107
Assessment reference	AN/3/3/1/1/34-i
Divisional Secretary's Division	Medawachchiya
Grama Niladhari Division where land/cultivated land is located	Akirikanda
Name of the village where land/cultivated land is located	Karapikkada

Dear Sir,

Proposed Anuradhapura-Vavunia-Mannar 220 kV Transmission Line
Clean Energy and Network Efficiency Improvement Project – Package 1
(Mannar Transmission Infrastructure Development Project)

Payment of Compensation

I hereby send you the signed payment voucher for the payment of compensation for the removal of trees/affected land. I am happy to receive the payment by cheque. Details of my bank account are given below.

Yours faithfully

Signature

National Identity Card No: **630313694V**

Name of the compensation
recipient/institution/religious place: **A S Jayasiri**

Bank Account No: **107630159930**

Address: **Karapikkada**
              Medawachchiya

Name of the bank:
National Savings Bank

Bank branch: **Medawachchiya**

[Official stamp of the institution]

වවුචර් අංකය	**ANVA/ME/AKR/107**
තක්සේරු යොමුව	අනු/3/3/1/1/34-i
පුාදේශීය ලේකම් කොට්ඨාශය	මැදවච්චිය
ඉඩම්/ වගා බිම පිහිටි ගුාම නිලධාරි කොට්ඨාශය	ඈකිරිකන්ද
ඉඩම්/ වගා බිම පිහිටි ගුාමයේ නාමය	කරපික්කඩ

වාාපෘති කළමණාකරු
සිරිඑන්ඊඅයිපී-81,
(මන්නාරම සම්පේෂණ යටිතල පහසුකම් වාාපෘතිය),
ලංකා විදුලිබල මණ්ඩලය,
35/2, පළමු මහල, උදයාන පාර,
මාබෝල, වත්තල.

මහත්මයාණෙනි,

යෝජිත අනුරාධපුර - වවුනියා - මන්නාරම ද.වෝ 220 විදුලි සම්පේෂණ මාර්ගය
පිරිතුරු බලශක්ති ජාලගත කාර්යක්ෂමතා වැඩිදියුණු කිරීමේ වාාපෘතිය - 01 වන පැ‍කේජය
(මන්නාරම සම්පේෂණ යටිතල පහසුකම්)

වන්දි මුදල් ගෙවීම

ඉඩමේ පිහිටි ගස් කැපීම්/ ඉඩමට සිදු වූ හානිය වෙනුවෙන් වන්දි මුදල් ගෙවීම සඳහා ඔබ විසින් එවන ලද වවුචරය අත්සන් කොට මේ සමග එවමි. වන්දි මුදල් චෙක්පතකින් ලබා ගැනීමට කැමැත්තෙමි. මාගේ බැංකු ගිණුම් විස්තර පහත සඳහන් පරිදි වේ.

මෙයට - විශ්වාසී

අත්සන

අත්සන ....

ජා. හැ. අංකය : 530313594v

වන්දි ලාභියාගේ / ආයතනයේ /: A.S ජයසිරි
පූජනීය ස්ථානයේ නම ....

ගිණුම් අංකය : 107630159930

ලිපිනය : කරපික්කඩ
මැදවච්චිය

බැංකුවේ නම : ජාතික ඉතිරි කිරීමේ බැංකුව

බැංකු ශාඛාව : මැදවච්චිය

P/b No: 080-57/P80/17/0377
18/07/17

ආයතනයේ නිල මුද්‍රාව : ....

Project Manager, CENEIP - P1
(Mannar Transmission Infrastructure Development Project)
Ceylon Electricity Board
35/2, First Floor, Park Road,
Mabole, Wattala

CEB Reference No.	PM/CENEIP-P1/ TE/20(D)
Voucher No.	ANVA/ME/AKR/107
Divisional Secretary's Division	Medawachchiya
Grama Niladhari Division where land/cultivated land is located	Akirikanda

Dear Sir,

Clean Energy and Network Efficiency Improvement
Project – Package 1
(Mannar Transmission Infrastructure Development Project)

Proposed Anuradhapura-Vavunia-Mannar 220 kV Transmission Line

Permission for Wayleave Clearance

Reference the letter No. PM/CENEIP-P1/TE/20 (D) dated .../.../.... and the enclosed request made in terms of para.3 of Schedule 1 of the Sri Lanka Electricity Act No.20 of 2009, I/We, A S Jayasiri, owner/occupant of the land located at Karapikkada, Medawachchiya hereby give permission for wayleave clearance subject to the receipt of compensation.

Thank you,

Yours faithfully,

Signature of the landowner/occupant

Date: 10.7.2017

(Note: delete the irrelevant words)

ලංවීම යොමු අංකය	PM/CENEIP-P1/TE/20(D)
වවුචර් අංකය	**ANVA/ME/AKR/107**
ප්‍රාදේශීය ලේකම් කොට්ඨාශය	මැදවච්චිය
ඉඩම/ වගා බිම පිහිටි ග්‍රාම නිලධාරී කොට්ඨාශය	ඇකිරිකන්ද

ව්‍යාපෘති කළමණාකරු
සිටීඑන්ඊඅයිපී-81,
(මන්නාරම සම්ප්‍රේෂණ යටිතල පහසුකම් ව්‍යාපෘතිය),
ලංකා විදුලිබල මණ්ඩලය,
35/2, පළමු මහල, උද්‍යාන පාර,
මාබෝල, වත්තල.

මහත්මයාණෙනි,

පිවිතුරු බලශක්ති ජාලගත කාර්යක්ෂමතා වැඩිදියුණු කිරීමේ ව්‍යාපෘතිය - 01 පැකේජය
(මන්නාරම සම්ප්‍රේෂණ යටිතල පහසුකම්)

යෝජිත අනුරාධපුර - වව්නියාව - මන්නාරම ද.වෝ 220 විදුලි සම්ප්‍රේෂණ මාර්ගය ඉදිකිරීම.

<u>මාර්ග අවසරය ලබා දීම.</u>

....

.... කරුස්තහඩ , මැදවච්චිය .... ලිපිනයේ පිහිටි ඉඩමේ
අයිතිකරු/පදිංචිකරු, නම).......A. S. ජයසිරි

වන මම/අපි ලංකා විදුලිබල මණ්ඩලයේ **PM/CE&NEIP-P1/TE/20(D)** හා ..../........./......... දිනැති ලිපිය
සමඟ එවන ලද 2009 අංක 20 දරණ ශ්‍රී ලංකා විදුලිබල පනතේ 1 වන උපලේඛණයේ 3 වැනි වගන්තිය අනුව නිකුත්
කරන ලද ඉල්ලීම පරිදි වන්දි මුදල් ලබා ගැනීම යටතේ මාර්ග අවසර ලබා දෙන බව මෙයින් දැනුම් දෙමි/ දෙමු.

ස්තුතියි,
ශ්‍රයට විශ්වාසී වූ,

....
ඉඩමේ අයිතිකරු/පදිංචිකරුගේ අත්සන

දිනය :..2017 . 07 . 10

(සටහන : අනවශ්‍ය වචන කපා හරින්න.)

Ceylon Electricity Board
(Established by Parliamentary Act No. 17 of 1969)

Location:	CENEIP – P1 (Mannar Transmission Infrastructure Development Project)Ceylon Electricity Board 35/2, First Floor, Park Road, Mabole, Wattala		Voucher No.	ANVA/ME/AKR/107
Cost centre:	980/57		Assessment reference	AN/3/3/1/1/34-i
Operations Division:	Project Manager CENEIP – P1 (Mannar Transmission Infrastructure Development Project)		Divisional Secretariat Division:	Medawachchiya
Name and address of the recipient of compensation:	A S Jayasiri Karapikkada Medawachchiya		Grama Niladhari Division where land/cultivated land is located	Akirikanda

Details	Amount (SLR)
Payment of compensation estimated by the Divisional Secretary, in terms of the provisions in Schedule 1 of Sri Lanka Electricity Act No.20 of 2009 for the above-mentioned land/cultivated land and per the details given in the over leaf:	51,750.00
Prepared by:	Signature
Checked by:	Signature

I, according to my knowledge and the relevant documents including details provided in the over leaf, certify that the above-mentioned task had been carried out with formal approvals, and the payment of Sri Lankan Rupees Fifty-One Thousand Seven Hundred Fifty is justifiable in terms of the regulations.

Signed:

Eng. W F M Fernando
Project Manager
CENEIP – P1
(Mannar Transmission Infrastructure Development Project)

Date: 20.7.2017

I certify that I have received the compensation payment of SLR51,750 entitled by me on 10.7.2017.

Name of the recipient of the cheque: A S Jayasiri

Signature:

National Identity Card No: 630313694V

ගෙවීම් වවුචරය
ලංකා විදුලිබල මණ්ඩලය
(1969 අංක 17 දරණ පාර්ලිමේන්තු පණතින් ස්ථාපිතයි)

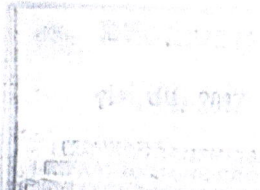

ස්ථානය	සිර්ඵන්ට්අයිසී-81, (මන්නාරම සම්ප්‍රේෂණ යටිතල පහසුකම් ව්‍යාපෘතිය), ලංකා විදුලිබල මණ්ඩලය, 35/2, පළමු මහල, උද්‍යාන පාර, මාබෝල, වත්තල.	වවුචර් අංකය	**ANVA/ME/AKR/107**
පිරිවැය මධ්‍යස්ථානය	980/57	තක්සේරු යොමුව	අනු/3/3/1/1/34-i
කාර්යය අංශය	ව්‍යාපෘති කළමණාකරු සිර්ඵන්ට්අයිසී-81, (මන්නාරම සම්ප්‍රේෂණ යටිතල පහසුකම් ව්‍යාපෘතිය),	ප්‍රාදේශීය ලේකම් කොට්ඨාශය	මැදවච්චිය
		ඉඩම්/ වගා බිම පිහිටි ග්‍රාම නිලධාරී කොට්ඨාශය	ඇකිරිකන්ද
වන්දි ලාභියාගේ නම සහ තැපැල් ලිපිනය	ඒ.එස්. ජයසිරි මයා කරපික්කඩ, මැදවච්චිය.	ඉඩම්/ වගා බිම පිහිටි ග්‍රාමයේ නාමය	කරපික්කඩ

විස්තරය	මුදල (රු.)	
අනුරාධපුර සිට මන්නාරම දක්වා වෙනියාව හරහා වූ ද. වෝ. 220 විදුලි සම්ප්‍රේෂණ මාර්ගය ඉදිකිරීමේදී 2009 අංක 20 දරණ ශ්‍රී ලංකා විදුලිබල පනතේ 01 වන උප ලේඛනය පරිදි මැදවච්චිය ප්‍රාදේශීය ලේකම් විසින් ගෙවීමට තක්සේරු කරන ලද ඉහත දක්වා ඇති ඉඩමට / වගාබිමට පසුපිටෙහි විස්තර සඳහන් අලාභහානි සඳහා වන්දි වශයෙන් කරනු ලබන ගෙවීමයි.	51,750	00
සකස් කළේ :		
පරීක්ෂා කළේ :		

ඉහත කී කාර්යය විධිමත් පරිදි අනුමතිය ඇතිව කරන ලද බවත් ඒ සඳහා රුපියල් පනස්එක්දහස් හත්සියපනහක් ගෙවීම, රෙගුලාසි වලට අනුකූලව සාධාරණ බවත් මාගේ දැනුම හා මීට අදාළ යොනු වල සහ පසු පිටෙහි දැක්වෙන කරුණු අනුවත් සහතික කරමි.

ඉංජිනේරු ඩබ්ලිව්.එල්.එම්. ප්‍රනාන්ද
ව්‍යාපෘති කළමණාකරු
සිර්ඵන්ට්අයිසී-81
(මන්නාරම සම්ප්‍රේෂණ යටිතල පහසුකම් ව්‍යාපෘතිය)

P/B අංක: 980-57/030/17/0977

දිනය : 25/7/2017

මෙම වන්දි මුදලේ හිමිකරු මම වන බව මෙයින් සහතික කරන අතර, රුපියල් ....51,750/1......
.... ක මුදල 2017.07.11 දින භාරගත් බවට සහතික කරමි.

වෙක්ෂ්පත භාරගත් අයගේ නම : A.S. ජයසිරි

අත්සන :

ජාතික හැඳුනුම්පත් අංකය : 630313094V

Ceylon Electricity Board
CENEIP – P1
(Mannar Transmission Infrastructure Development Project)

Proposed Anuradhapura-Vavunia-Mannar 220 kV Transmission Line

Payment of compensation for land/cultivated land affected by transmission line in terms of the provisions in Schedule 1 of Sri Lanka Electricity Act No.20 of 2009

Ref No.	Nature of the damage	Unit rate (SLR)	Quantity	Amount (SLR)
	Hik 1'	500	4	2,000
	Hoorimara 1.5'	1,750	3	5,250
	Hoorimara 1'	1,000	1	1.000
	Hoorimara 3'	5,500	2	11,000
	Hoorimara 2'	4,000	2	8,000
	Burutha 1'	2,000	1	2,000
	Maila 1'	1,000	4	4,000
	Hoorimara 4.5'	7,500	1	7,500
	Koon 7.5'	7,250	1	7,250
	Kaduru 1.5'	750	1	750
	Kaduru 1'	500	6	3,000
Sri Lankan Rupees Fifty One Thousand Seven Hundred Fifty				**51,750**

I/We, the lawful owners of the land, hereby agree to grant permission for the wayleave clearance including the entry to the land belonging to me/us (details of which are provided in the over leaf), for the construction and operation of the transmission line inside this land, its inspection, maintenance, alterations, and rehabilitation, subject to the payment of compensation due to me/us by the Ceylon Electricity Board for the land affected by the construction of the Anuradhapura-Vavunia-Mannar 220 kV Transmission Line. I/We, also certify that as instructed, I/we have removed and cleared the trees that would obstruct the transmission line.

Name/s of the landowner: A S Jayasiri

National Identify Card No: 630313694V

Signature:

Date:

Recommend the certified payment of compensation	Recommend and forward for approval
Electrical Superintendent/Date/Official Stamp	Electrical Engineer/Date/Official Stamp

ලංකා විදුලිබල මණ්ඩලය

සිරිඑන්ටීඅයිපි-පී1 (මන්නාරම සම්ප්‍රේෂණ යටිතල පහසුකම් ව්‍යාපෘතිය)

යෝජිත අනුරාධපුර - වවුනියාව - මන්නාරම ද.වෝ 220 විදුලි සම්ප්‍රේෂණ මාර්ගය

2009 අංක 20 දරණ ශ්‍රී ලංකා විදුලිබල පනතේ 01 වන උප ලේඛනය යටතේ
විදුලි සම්ප්‍රේෂණ මාර්ගයේ බලපෑමට ලක්වන ඉඩම් / වගාබිම් සඳහා වන්දි ගෙවීම.

යොමුව	හානියේ ස්වභාවය	ඒකකය		ප්‍රමාණය	මුළු මුදල	
		රු.	ශත		රු.	ශත
	තීක් 1'	500	00	04	2,000	00
	හූරි මාර 1.5'	1,750	00	03	5,250	00
	හූරි මාර 1'	1,000	00	01	1,000	00
	හූරි මාර 3'	5,500	00	02	11,000	00
	හූරි මාර 2'	4,000	00	02	8,000	00
	බුරුත 1'	2,000	00	01	2,000	00
	මයිල 1'	1,000	00	04	4,000	00
	හූරි මාර 4.5'	7,500	00	01	7,500	00
	කෝන් 7.5'	7,250	00	01	7,250	00
	කූරරු 1.5'	750	00	01	750	00
	කූරරු 1'	500	00	06	3,000	00
රුපියල් පනස්එක්දහස් හත්සියපනහක් පමණි					51,750	00

Approved for Payment
Amount Rs: 51,750/-
Project Manager
(CE&NTIP-P1)

මා / අප විසින් නීත්‍යානුකූලව හිමිකම් කියනු ලබන මාගේ / අපගේ ඉඩම මතින් අනුරාධපුර සිට මන්නාරම දක්වා වවුනියාව
හරහා දූ ද.වෝ. 220 විදුලි සම්ප්‍රේෂණ මාර්ගයේ ඉදිකිරීම් කටයුතු කරගෙන යාමේදී වන හානි සඳහා ඉහත දක්වා ඇති
වන්දි මුදල ලංකා විදුලිබල මණ්ඩලය මගින් මා / අප වෙත ගෙවීමේ කොන්දේසියට යටත්ව, එම විදුලි සම්ප්‍රේෂණ මාර්ගය මා
හට / අප හට අයත් පසු පිවිසි විස්තර කර ඇති ඉඩම් තුළ ඉදිකර පවත්වා ගෙන යාම, එම විදුලි සම්ප්‍රේෂණ මාර්ගයේ පරීක්ෂා
කිරීම, නඩත්තු කිරීම, සැකසීම සහ අලුත්වැඩියා කිරීමේ කටයුතු සඳහා ඉඩමට ඇතුල්වීමේ අයිතිය ඇතුළත් "මාර්ග අවසරය"
ලබා දීමට එකඟ වෙමු. විදුලි සම්ප්‍රේෂණ මාර්ගයට බාධා විය හැකි නිසා කපා / ගලවා ඉවත් කරන ලෙසට දන්වා තිබූ සියලු
ගස් කපා / ගලවා ඉවත් කර ඇති බව ද මෙයින් තහවුරු කරමි / කරමු.

ඉඩම් හිමියා / හිමියන්ගේ නම : A S ජයසිරි

ජාතික හැඳුනුම්පත් අංකය : 630319674V

අත්සන : X

දිනය :

P/3 NO: 960-57/PI/17/03-17
18/07/17

සහතික කර ඇති අලාභහානි සඳහා ගෙවීම් නිර්දේශ කරමි.

...... 20/06/2017

විදුලි අධිකාරි අත්සන / දිනය / නිල මුද්‍රාව :

නිර්දේශ කර අනුමැතිය සඳහා ඉදිරිපත් කරමි.

17/07/2017

විදුලි ඉංජිනේරු අත්සන / දිනය / නිල මුද්‍රාව :

7. Thulhiriya–Kegalle 132-Kilovolt Transmission Line Cases

This appendix presents some cases based on the review of written complaints from affected persons (APs).

Case No. 1: The AP submitted several complaints to the district parliamentarian, deputy minister of power and energy, project manager of Ceylon Electricity Board (CEB), and the President of Sri Lanka which contained the following grievances.

- The transmission line was planned to traverse his 3-story house, and as a result, both his business premises (a coconut oil manufacturing mill and a rice mill) and the house are in insecure status causing risks to their lives.

- He had obtained a bank loan for his business and a lease agreement for lorry. He had actually paid a monthly loan installment of SLR78,000. The loan had been taken by mortgaging his land to the bank, and installation of the transmission line over this land would result in the devaluation of his property as well as the future development of his business.

- The Divisional Secretary had given permission to erect the transmission line over the road between two houses, but the line was now constructed against the decision of the secretary.

- The original route was planned over paddy fields and barren land for which the villagers had given their written consent. However, subsequently, people settled down in these lands and thus, raised their objections to installing a transmission line over their houses. In response to these objections, CEB changed the route at an additional cost of SLR15 million. Neither CEB nor the Divisional Secretary had prevented the people from constructing houses on the land earmarked for the transmission line.

- During field inspections by the Divisional Secretary and the Assistant Divisional Secretary, the AP tried to show documents citing his losses resulting from the construction of the transmission line, but none of them were seriously considered.

- The new route would lead to the removal of around 50 coconut trees and a few jackfruit trees. Moreover, the AP would not be able to plant tall trees in his land.

- Removal of trees would cause running out of water fountains and destruction of cultivations.

- His source of livelihood is coconut cultivation and cutting down of coconut trees would lead to loss of his livelihood and incomes, making him vulnerable to poverty.

- The AP was of the view that the Divisional Secretary and CEB held conflicting views and felt that they did not listen to the people and made one-sided decisions.

The following were the actions taken to address the complaints:
- The deputy minister of Power and Renewable Energy directed the general manager of CEB to consider an alternate route for the line.

- The Divisional Secretary offered compensation for the devaluation of his land as well as for the trees to be removed.

The complainant was informed by the Divisional Secretary that the line route could not be changed as it was the least-impacted route.

Dissatisfied with the response he received, the AP sought legal action in courts, the case of which is described in Appendix 8. Finally, the AP agreed to accept a cash compensation package from the project for his losses which amounted to SLR6.27 million. This compensation included SLR5.46 million for the devaluation of his property caused by the transmission line that was erected on his land, house, and another building, and SLR810,300 for the loss of his 23 fruit-bearing trees and 7 timber trees.

Case No. 2: The AP complained to the regional office of the Human Rights Commission and the following grievances were reported.
- The change of the original route by CEB caused removal of all the trees in his property.

- Removal of vegetation would make it difficult for him to live in his house.

- He had mortgaged his land and had obtained a loan of SLR1 million to invest in anthurium flower cultivation and a greenhouse for seedlings as his source of livelihood. Removal of the trees affected his greenhouse and the flower plants, and he would not be able to repay the loan.

- Transmission line will cause life risks and dangers to the members of his family.

- He is living in ill health and this will cause their lives to be vulnerable.

The AP agreed to accept the compensation package provided by the project which included SLR277,900 for the construction of two alternative greenhouses, each with a floor area of 36 feet by 17 feet; SLR9,000 for the loss of one timber tree, and another SLR1.95 million for the devaluation of his land due to the installation of the transmission line in his property. The total compensation package amounted to SLR2.24 million.

Case No. 3: The AP, together with 48 villagers (footnote 1), complained to the Prime Minister and the President of Sri Lanka reporting the following grievances.
- The villagers were dependent on casual labor work and each household owned only 15-20 perches of land. Their only source of drinking water source were the wells. The removal of trees would dry the wells and would destroy their properties.
- They requested that the transmission line be installed over paddy fields and in areas where there were no settlements.
- The villagers feared that the transmission line would endanger their lives and damage their properties.
- The line would affect around 50 households.

The total compensation package that the AP received from the project amounted to SLR1.45 million. This comprised SLR1.21 million for the devaluation of his property by the transmission line crossing over his land, and another SLR237,750 for the loss of 23 fruit-bearing trees and 12 timber trees.

Case No. 4: The AP complained to the President of Sri Lanka and reported the following.
- He was already 63 years old and was a poor farmer, not receiving any government subsidies, but was dependent on cultivations.
- Transmission line will result in the removal of about 80 rubber trees and damage his pepper, coconut, goraka, arecanut, jackfruit, and other timber trees.
- The line will traverse close to his house.
- He was taken to the police station for questioning. He had never been to a police station.
- He requested CEB to consider an alternate route.

The AP was compensated for his losses in the amount of SLR2.30 million including SLR2 million for the loss of his trees, and another SLR299,316 for devaluation of his land. The number of trees that had to be removed by the AP was 255 comprising 108 timber trees, 132 fruit-bearing trees, and 15 pepper wines.

Case No. 5: The AP complained to the project manager of CEB with the following:
- He had no objections to the transmission line.

- He needed higher compensation for the rubber trees to be removed from his land. The CEB earlier agreed to pay SLR12,000 for a rubber tree based on its productivity cycle. He was then informed that compensation for a tree will be around SLR3,900 to SLR4,000 for each.

- He would not allow any construction work of the transmission line over his property nor would he remove the trees until appropriate compensation was paid to him.

The AP subsequently accepted a compensation package of SLR1.40 million which included SLR844,116 for the loss of 92 timber trees, 6 fruit-bearing trees, and 16 bamboo bushes; SLR300,423 for devaluation of his land due to the transmission line; and another SLR258,000 for the land lost for the base of a tower.

Case No. 6: The AP complained to the project manager of CEB with the following:
- The trees planted on his land were earmarked for removal without his knowledge.

- Someone had prepared a false deed for this land and tried to remove the trees. He had complained to the police and the removal of trees was halted.

The dispute between the two parties over land titles could not be resolved despite attempts made by the project and the Divisional Secretary. The project implementation in this section was delayed due to the failure to remove the trees. In these circumstances, the project advised both parties to resolve the issue between them, remove the trees, and report to the project for payment of the compensation due them. Meanwhile, the party who was allegedly holding a false deed took action to remove the trees, and reported to the project after. The AP neither raised objections nor complained to the Divisional Secretary or the police against the party that removed the trees. The project decided to pay compensation to the person who removed the trees in the amount of SLR2.08 million. The compensation package included SLR1.77 million for the loss of 170 timber trees and 52 fruit-bearing trees; SLR298,541 for land devaluation due to transmission line; and another SLR10,000 for the land lost for the base of the transmission tower.

8. Court Cases

Case No. 1: In one place of the right of way, conductors were planned to be erected between two houses. But the two households objected. One of the affected persons (APs) filed a case against the Ceylon Electricity Board (CEB) in the Magistrate's Court. The court issued an injunction order preventing the construction work for 3 months in the disputed section. As a result, CEB decided to acquire the wayleave. Despite the court case and the land acquisition process, negotiations with the landowner continued to get his consent for the line route. CEB requested the AP to produce a valuation report for his affected property, but what he produced was a valuation report for his entire land which was not acceptable. Due to objections from the two APs and obstructions to work teams, there was not much space for exploring alternatives to avoid impacts on structures. As a result, the conductors traversed part of the roof of one AP for which the compensation was paid by CEB.

Case No. 2: The AP was to receive a good compensation package for his affected property including his affected trees. However, he was not willing to accept compensation but instead, filed a case with the District Appeal Court. The Court was of the opinion that the transmission line could not be proscribed because of its national importance. Thereafter, he appealed to the Court of Appeal in Colombo against land acquisition. At this time, Section 38(a) under the Land Acquisition Act had been issued. The section allows the acquiring officer to take over the immediate possession of the land for urgent reasons and pending the payment of compensation. The Court of Appeal did not issue an injunction order. CEB was ready with a valuation report and the Divisional Secretary informed the AP to hand over his property under the provisions of Section 38(a). The AP continued his obstructions to land surveying, but later consented on the advice of his lawyer. Finally, he agreed to withdraw the court case and accept the compensation which was about SLR6 million, an amount higher than the government compensation. Moreover, CEB allowed him to remove his trees. Acquisition process was divested and this delayed his compensation by 6 months.